Planta, How to Select a Bow for Violin Family Instruments

978-0093-

AF005931

978-0933-2243-15

BALTHASAR PLANTA

How to Select a Bow for Violin Family Instruments

ZÜRICH/EMBRACH
1981

Introduction

The world of music would lose much of its colour if there were no stringed instruments. However, the sound of string music could be made even more enjoyable if the three parameters involved in its production — performer, instrument and bow — could be properly matched to one another.

Co-ordinating these three parameters produces an entity that gives satisfaction and pleasure. When great musicians — violinists, violists or cellists — are heard and observed one is constantly fascinated by the relaxed way they play; performer, instrument and bow are in perfect harmony with one another. This dynamic equilibrium is not solely the product of musical talent and intensive practice but demands additionally both comprehension of the human being centrally involved and an instrument and bow matched to him.

I have devoted many years to studying the design of stringed instruments and bows and feel the urge to pass on what I have learnt as a contribution to the literature on bows*, which is relatively sparse by comparison with the wealth of material that has been written about stringed instruments. I hope that my researches will contribute to improving stringed performers' understanding of bows as a parameter and help them to enrich their playing by ensuring that they use a suitable bow. In addition, it is my hope that makers and collectors of bows will also find something of interest in this book.

* Bows for Musical Instruments by Joseph Roda. — Les archets français par Etienne Vatelot. — J. B. Vuillaume, His Life and Work by Hill/Millant. — How to make a violin bow by Frank V. Henderson. — Die Kunst des Geigenbaues von Möckel-Winckel. — Die Physiologie der Bogenführung von Streichinstrumenten von Dr. F. A. Steinhausen. — Der Geigenbogen: Ratschläge für alle Geiger von Friedrich Wunderlich. — Manuel Pratique de Lutherie, par Roger et Max Millant.

The Bow: The Third Parameter

I do not propose to deal here with the general historical develop-
ment of the bow, but one basic design cannot be left out of
account, namely that described by François Tourte (1747—1835)
in his writings. Bow manufacture calls for an entirely different
basic training from that of a violin maker, and for this reason bow
making must be regarded as a special field of instrument making.
Few violin makers are known to have been as skilled in making
bows as they were in fashioning their instruments. François Tourte
collaborated with string players of his day to design bows that
have remained yardsticks up to the present day and are veritable
works of art to delight musicians and collectors alike. Similarly,
Tourte was the first bow maker to draw attention to the unrivalled
suitability of Pernambuco wood as a material for bows and to use
that wood in practice. As we progress towards an ideal bow, we
shall seek hereunder to explore the elementary laws that lead
step by step via the theory of materials to the design and appraisal
of a good bow.

The Features of the Bow

It is common knowledge that a good bow is just as important as a
good instrument to a string player. However, many people are
not clear about the features that a good bow should have.
In addition to perfect materials and painstaking craftsmanship, a
good bow must basically display ideal weight distribution, an
ideally located centre of gravity and good elasticity combined
with great stability and resistance. Furthermore, a bow must retain
its properties of elasticity, resistance and enduring hardness for
years, even if subjected to intensive use. Over and above this, the

material utilized should not shrink much, even when air temperature and humidity fluctuate widely. And last but not least it must have an attractive appearance.

To make the foregoing observations quite clear, I will now describe the structure of a bow, which remains basically the same whether it is for use with a violin, viola, cello or double bass. It consists of the following elements:

a) the stick including the head
b) the device for tensioning the hair, known as a frog
c) the hair

These are the three most important elements, and those which are of relevance to the following study.

The Stick

Early bow makers utilized a number of varieties of wood which more or less fulfilled the necessary requirements. They included the following:

Red ironwood (Lophira procera);
Burma yellowheart (Fagraea fragrans);
Campeche (Haematoxylon campechianum);
European beech (Fagus silvatica);
European cherry (Prunus avium);
Wamara (Swartzia tomentosa);
Snakewood (Piratinera guianensis);
Tatajuba (Chlorophora tinctoria).

However, none of these varieties met the requirements of a first-class stick, and it was François Tourte whose protracted experiments led to the discovery of a material that fulfilled his stringent demands.

Translator's Note: These English names are the equivalents of the Latin botanical species given in the German text. They do not always coincide with the translations of the German names used.

In earlier times, dyeworks used coloured woods from Brazil, and sugar from that country was also imported in timber barrels. Tourte made tests with wood from these sources, and finally came upon the variety known as Brazilwood, Pernambuco wood or violinbow wood, a Guilandia sub-species of the Caesalpinia family.

The Guilandia is highly suitable for making bows, and should not be confused with other types of wood often known commercially as "Brazilwood", which may often be bulletwood or massaranduba — far less suitable for making bows. Since World War II, Pernambuco wood has mostly been obtained from the regions to the South of Rio de Janeiro and to the North of Recife. Pernambuco Province is in fact outside this area, and it is no longer clear whether it ever was a major source of Pernambuco wood, since extensive areas of Brazil have been deforested. As a matter of interest, the authorities no longer permit Pernambuco wood to be exported in the form of complete trunks, and only sawn planks are obtainable.

The bows Tourte made of Pernambuco wood were masterpieces, for he was an expert in appraising materials in addition to being a supreme craftsman. Bearing in mind that only about 8–10% of a shipment of Pernambuco wood is suitable for high-quality bows, the great value of Tourte's work can be recognized. His researches into materials suitable for making bows lead him to be regarded as the father of that great French dynasty of bow makers that includes such famous names as Peccate, Henri, Eury, Voirin, Lamy, Satory and many other worthy disciples of Tourte's skills. Henry Saint George and the Frenchman Vuillaume recognized that Tourte's bow designs were based on certain defined laws and attempted to express these in mathematical formulae, to which we shall be referring in a later chapter.

To sum up, it may be said that to make a good bow of Pernambuco wood only selected timber that has been impeccably stored and kept dry for years should be used. It follows that the price of such timber is very high. Depending on the characteristics of the wood, the skilled bow maker will have to modify the generalized laws to take account of the fact that wood is a natural product which may have very different characteristics of structure and quality, even within one and the same trunk or plank. It may be said without exaggeration that a good bow maker must have just as much creativity and craftsmanship as a good violin maker.

The Functions of the Bow

A bow is a device wielded by the right arm and hand of the player to cause the strings of his instrument to vibrate and thus produce sounds. The great importance of the interplay between the bow and bowing technique in producing a predetermined sound effect without generating cramp has been dealt with in detail from a doctor's and violinist's standpoint in Dr. F. A. Steinhausen's "Die Physiologie der Bogenführung von Streichinstrumenten". A careful study of this book reveals the importance of the bow as a parameter in trouble-free playing. Teachers of string playing consequently attach ever-increasing importance to correct bowing and bow grip.

Let us now consider, taking consistent note of Dr. Steinhausen's ideas in conjunction with Tourte's design principles, a concept for a bow corresponding as closely as possible to the ideal. Obviously, an idealized design like this could never be adopted in practice without reservations, since the bow maker must take account of heterogeneous characteristics in his material and use his skills to correct them. But before we address this question, let us first take note of the commonest bow dimensions.

According to various sources in the literature, François Tourte (1747—1835) fixed his bow lengths as follows:
Violin Bow
Length of stick, including head and screw   74—75 cm
Viola Bow
Length of stick, including head and screw   74 cm

Cello Bow
Length of stick, including head and screw   72−73 cm
It is open to question whether these are really the measurements as fixed by Tourte, as the metric system was not defined by the Paris Academy until 1799 and was only introduced by law in 1840.

Both French and Italian bow makers basically utilized the following measurements:

Violin Bow
Length of stick and head, less screw   73 cm
Weight of complete bow   55−65 g
Viola Bow
Length of stick and head, less screw   72 cm
Weight of complete bow   65−70 g
Cello Bow
Length of stick and head, less screw   69.5 cm
Weight of complete bow   70−80 g

The foregoing data are listed for orientation purposes only and provide no criterion as to quality.

For the purposes of our own study, let us adopt the following dimensions:
Violin Bow
Length of stick and head, less screw   73 cm
Weight of bow   60 g
Distance between bow end and centre of gravity max. 24−25 cm
Viola Bow
Length of stick and head, less screw   72 cm
Weight of bow   67 g
Distance between bow end and centre of gravity max. 24−25 cm
Cello Bow
Length of stick and head, less screw   69.5 cm

Weight of bow   75 g
Distance between bow end and centre of gravity max. 23−24 cm

The following specification may be adopted for designing an ideal bow:
a) Stable, parallel-grained, well-seasoned, dry Pernambuco wood
b) Stick length as prescribed
c) Bow weight as prescribed
d) Centre of gravity as prescribed

The following sketch illustrates how a bow may be considered as a two-armed lever whose fulcrum is located where the player's thumb and middle finger grasp the frog (point a). The index finger bears on the bow at point p and the little finger at point e. This method of gripping the bow has been regarded as most appropriate up to the present.

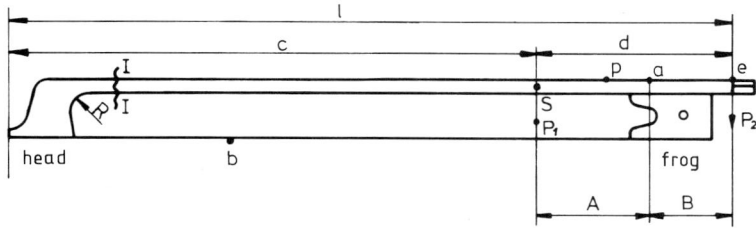

Explanation of symbols in the foregoing sketch:
l   = length of bow from head to end of stick, exclusive of screw
d   = distance between bow centre of gravity and stick end
a   = fulcrum at the point where the frog is gripped between the thumb and middle finger
b   = contact point between bow and string
S   = centre of gravity of bow
p   = point where index finger bears on bow
e   = point where little finger bears on bow

I–I = critical bow fracture point under hair tension plus playing tension
R   = head radius
P_1 = bow weight
P_2 = force of little finger

A calculation of the ideal moments for ideal bow control produces the following result:

$$P_1 \cdot A = P_2 \cdot B = \text{constant},$$

and indicates that the figure for a good bow needs to be specific. If, for example, the centre of gravity of the bow is displaced by faulty design towards the head, the bow will become top-heavy. And although in principle this disadvantage can be corrected by increasing the pressure of the little finger, the result is heavy hand fatigue and cramp. On the other hand, if the centre of gravity is too close to the fulcrum a, the bow will begin to jump uncontrollably during certain types of stroke. On the basis of the leverage law stated it is possible to determine a theoretical curve of moment permitting the adoption of similar conditions relating to ideal distribution of bow weight. The following figure shows a curve of this kind drawn for a violin bow with a weight of 60 g and a distance of 24 cm between centre of gravity and the end of the stick (less screw), the stick length being 73 cm. This curve can also be of practical use, especially for testing whether an existing bow has the correct weight distribution.

The equation corresponding to this curve (whose deduction I do not propose to reproduce here, since it is of little use to practitioners) is as follows:

$$Y = \frac{2.544}{1000} \cdot X^3 - \frac{1.118}{10} \cdot X^2 + \frac{6.948}{10} \cdot X + 17{,}538$$

If the length of the bow in cm is inserted for X, the product of the foregoing equation (Y) is the force or weight in grammes.

Theoretical moment curve related to fulcrum a

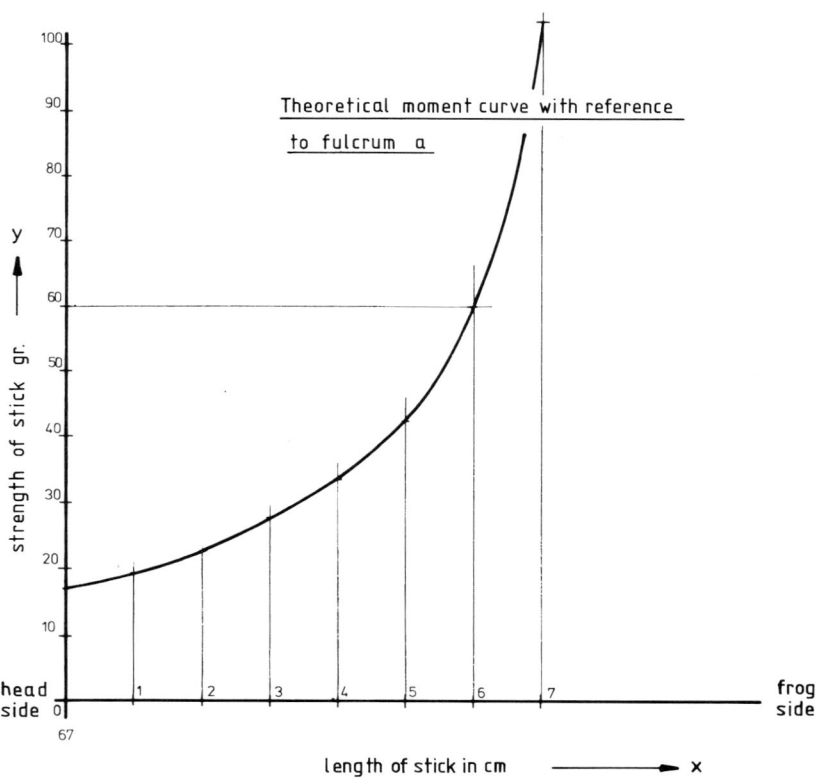

Theoretical moment curve with reference to fulcrum a

y — strength of stick gr.

x — length of stick in cm

head side

frog side

Determination of Bow Cross-section
on the Saint George and Vuillaume Principle

Before dealing with this method in detail, it is essential to point out the need for a minimum stick cross-section at the transition point between stick and head, in the light of the bending stresses

13

that occur at the head. Failure to take account of this will materially reduce the working life of the stick.

Let us consider Figure 1. It will be seen from this that a bending stress occurs at section I–I, partly due to the tensioning of the bow hairs and partly due to the supplementary forces applied when the violin is played. This is a critical cross-section, and it is here that a danger of fracture arises. Only painstaking head design and an appropriate radius R can reduce this danger. At this critical point, the quality of the bow wood becomes particularly important, and it is essential for the graining of the wood to be as fine as possible and above all parallel. It should also be borne in mind that stick diameter should under no circumstances be less than 5 mm (for a violin bow) at this critical point, as otherwise the bow will have a reduced working life. Some of the dimensions of famous Tourte bows are given hereunder. The measurements are taken from the periodical "The Strad" for August 1972, supplemented by other figures given the author by the Henry Ford Museum, Dearborn.

The Rochefoucauld
Stick thickness at frog   8.6 mm
Stick thickness at head   5.3 mm
Octagonal stick
Length of stick including head but excluding screw   723.5 mm

The Balakovic 1790
Stick thickness at frog   8.7 mm
Stick thickness at head   5.55 mm
Stick round
Length of stick including head but excluding screw   720.5 mm

The Sartory about 1780
Stick thickness at frog   8.7 mm
Stick thickness at head   4.9 mm

14

Stick round
Length of stick including head but excluding screw   720.7 mm

The Esterhazy ca. 1790
Stick thickness at frog   7.5 mm
Stick thickness at head   4.8 mm
Stick round
Length of stick including head but excluding screw   725.5 mm

The Vieuxtemps ca. 1800
Stick thickness at frog   7.5 mm
Stick thickness at head   5.55 mm
Octagonal stick
Length of stick including head but excluding screw   725.5 mm

The Nachez ca. 1810
Stick thickness at frog   7.5 mm
Stick thickness at head   4.8 mm
Octagonal stick
Length of stick including head but excluding screw   725.5 mm

The Baron de Tremont
Stick thickness at frog   8.55 mm
Stick thickness at head   5.55 mm
Octagonal stick
Length of stick including head but excluding screw   728.3 mm

It emerges from this comparison of dimensions that Tourte gradually began to use longer sticks as he grew older, finally approaching 730 mm. Departures from the predictable stick diameter at the head end can also be observed, but these are most likely due to differences in the qualities of the Pernambuco wood used, since hard, elastic wood requires different treatment from material that is relatively soft and heavy. The specific gravity of

Pernambuco wood varies between limits of about $0.80-0.97\,\mathrm{g/cm^3}$. Tourte was, as we have already seen, a great connoisseur of wood and applied his knowledge expertly to his bow designs. The following example compares the stick rigidity figures of round and octagonal bow sections by comparing their section moduli for a given stick cross-section, thus supporting the foregoing observations.

Section modulus is a very important factor in theoretical mechanics. The cross-section must be so determined that the safe material stresses for an applied flexural force are not exceeded, as otherwise there will be permanent deformation of the bow or even a fracture. For a round section, section modulus W is defined as follows:

$$W = \frac{\pi}{32} \cdot d^3$$

or approximately $0.1 \cdot d^3$, where d is the diameter of the circular cross-section.

For an octangular section the equation is more complicated, and space does not permit it to be worked through here.

Round Section   *Octagonal Section*

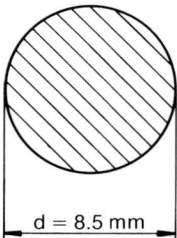

d = 8.5 mm

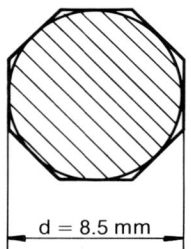

d = 8.5 mm

$$W = \frac{\pi}{32} \cdot 0.85^3 = 0.0603\,\mathrm{cm^3}$$

16

Theoretical section modulus W = 0.07010 cm^3.

The difference between the two section moduli is thus:

$$W = 0.07010 - 0.0603$$
$$= 0.00984 \text{ cm}^3$$

or expressed as a percentage:

$$\frac{0.00984}{0.0701} \cdot 100 = 15\%.$$

It will be seen from the foregoing example that given the same dimensions a stick of octagonal section has greater flexural strength than a round one. It is probably because of this fact that experienced bow makers prefer to keep the stick round when working in wood with a high specific gravity, and this is particularly the case where a very rigid Pernambuco wood is concerned. In other words, a bow maker has complete freedom to match the most suitable cross-section to the material in hand and thus produce an optimum bow.

Determination of Stick Section Along its Length

The average length of a violin bow stick is about 700 mm, excluding the head. Over a length of 110 mm from the frog end the stick is absolutely cylindrical. From that point onwards, stick cross-section reduces in geometrical progression. For the example hereunder, let stick diameter be 8.55 mm at the cylindrical portion and 5.55 mm at the head. J. B. Vuillaume, the French violin and bow maker, established a rule under which the cross-section of the bow stick must reduce along the stick axis to come as close as possible to the dimensions adopted by Tourte in the light of his empirical results.

17

Violin Bow

Diameter of stick cylindrical portion   8.55 mm
Diameter of stick at head   <u>5.55 mm</u>
Difference in diameter   <u>3.00 mm</u>

These 3 mm are spread among 10 points along the stick length of $700 - 110 = 590$ mm. As a result, stick diameter reduction between two points is 0.3 mm. However, the intervals between points along the 590 mm of the stick axis are not regular, but vary in accordance with a geometrical progression.

The following diagram illustrates the principle for fixing the diameter of the stick along its length. It should be mentioned additionally that in practice the best procedure is to erect a perpendicular at each end of a horizontal line 700 mm long. The perpendicular will measure 110 mm at the frog end and 21.5 mm at the head end. The cylindrical portion of the stick is 110 mm long. If this distance is measured off horizontally to the right from the frog end, it brings us to point A_0. At point A_0 erect a perpendicular 110 mm long. This point is marked 0 in the diagram. The head end of the stick is marked A_{10} and the other end of the perpendicular 21.5 mm long erected there is marked 10. A line is now drawn to connect 0 and 10, after which the distance $A_0 - 0$ is set on a pair of compasses and an arc drawn to point A_1. Here again a perpendicular is erected. The point of intersection between this perpendicular and the line connecting $0 - 10$ is point 1. Once again, this distance is set on the compasses and an arc drawn to point A_2. The procedure is then continued until point 10 is reached.

Violin Bow   ▶

J. B. Vuillaume's design principle
Stick length excluding head   700 mm
Stick diameter at cylindrical portion   8.55 mm
Stick diameter at head   5.55 mm

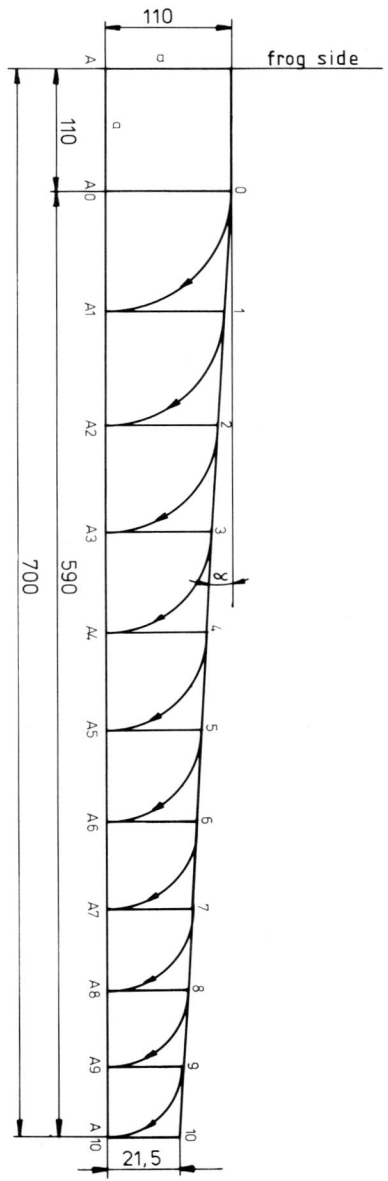

From point 0 to point 10, stick diameter reduces by 0.3 mm from point to point.

It is easy to see the geometrical rule illustrated by the foregoing figure. It is as follows:

$$a + a(1-tg\alpha) + a(1-tg\alpha)^2 + a(1-tg\alpha)^3 + \ldots a(1-tg\alpha)^9 = 590$$
Substitution: let $(1-tg) = q$

This produces a substitution rule as follows:

$$1 + q + q^2 + q^3 + q^4 + q^5 + q^6 + q^7 + q^8 + q^9 = 5.7676$$

The sum of this series is as follows:

$$S = \frac{1-q^{10}}{1-q} = 5.3636$$

The solution of this equation, by means of the false position rule, produces the following:

$$q = 0.850$$
Now $q = 1-tg\alpha \cdot tg\alpha = 1-q = 0.15$

In the light of the foregoing considerations, there result the following stick dimensions which, for greater clarity, are shown in tabular form.

Violin Bow

Measured points	Distance along stick in mm	Stick diameter in mm
A	0	8.55
A_0	110	8.55
A_1	220	8.25

20

Theoretical section modulus $W = 0.07010$ cm^3.

The difference between the two section moduli is thus:

$$W = 0.07010 - 0.0603$$
$$= 0.00984 \text{ cm}^3$$

or expressed as a percentage:

$$\frac{0.00984}{0.0701} \cdot 100 = 15\%.$$

It will be seen from the foregoing example that given the same dimensions a stick of octagonal section has greater flexural strength than a round one. It is probably because of this fact that experienced bow makers prefer to keep the stick round when working in wood with a high specific gravity, and this is particularly the case where a very rigid Pernambuco wood is concerned. In other words, a bow maker has complete freedom to match the most suitable cross-section to the material in hand and thus produce an optimum bow.

Determination of Stick Section Along its Length

The average length of a violin bow stick is about 700 mm, excluding the head. Over a length of 110 mm from the frog end the stick is absolutely cylindrical. From that point onwards, stick cross-section reduces in geometrical progression. For the example hereunder, let stick diameter be 8.55 mm at the cylindrical portion and 5.55 mm at the head. J. B. Vuillaume, the French violin and bow maker, established a rule under which the cross-section of the bow stick must reduce along the stick axis to come as close as possible to the dimensions adopted by Tourte in the light of his empirical results.

Violin Bow

Diameter of stick cylindrical portion	8.55 mm
Diameter of stick at head	5.55 mm
Difference in diameter	3.00 mm

These 3 mm are spread among 10 points along the stick length of $700 - 110 = 590$ mm. As a result, stick diameter reduction between two points is 0.3 mm. However, the intervals between points along the 590 mm of the stick axis are not regular, but vary in accordance with a geometrical progression.

The following diagram illustrates the principle for fixing the diameter of the stick along its length. It should be mentioned additionally that in practice the best procedure is to erect a perpendicular at each end of a horizontal line 700 mm long. The perpendicular will measure 110 mm at the frog end and 21.5 mm at the head end. The cylindrical portion of the stick is 110 mm long. If this distance is measured off horizontally to the right from the frog end, it brings us to point A_0. At point A_0 erect a perpendicular 110 mm long. This point is marked 0 in the diagram. The head end of the stick is marked A_{10} and the other end of the perpendicular 21.5 mm long erected there is marked 10. A line is now drawn to connect 0 and 10, after which the distance $A_0 - 0$ is set on a pair of compasses and an arc drawn to point A_1. Here again a perpendicular is erected. The point of intersection between this perpendicular and the line connecting $0 - 10$ is point 1. Once again, this distance is set on the compasses and an arc drawn to point A_2. The procedure is then continued until point 10 is reached.

Violin Bow ▶

J. B. Vuillaume's design principle
Stick length excluding head   700 mm
Stick diameter at cylindrical portion   8.55 mm
Stick diameter at head   5.55 mm

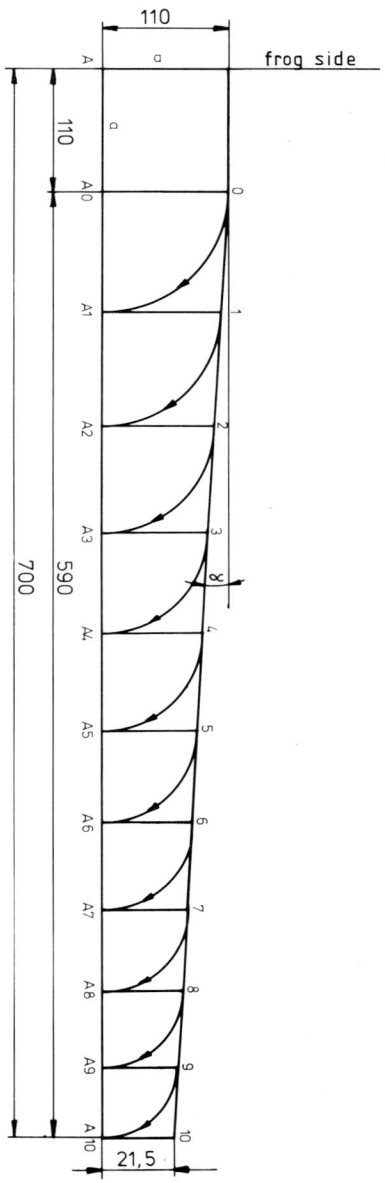

frog side

From point 0 to point 10, stick diameter reduces by 0.3 mm from point to point.

It is easy to see the geometrical rule illustrated by the foregoing figure. It is as follows:

$$a + a(1-\text{tg}\alpha) + a(1-\text{tg}\alpha)^2 + a(1-\text{tg}\alpha)^3 + \ldots a(1-\text{tg}\alpha)^9 = 590$$
$$\textit{Substitution: } \text{let } (1-\text{tg}) = q$$

This produces a substitution rule as follows:

$$1 + q + q^2 + q^3 + q^4 + q^5 + q^6 + q^7 + q^8 + q^9 = 5.7676$$

The sum of this series is as follows:

$$S = \frac{1-q^{10}}{1-q} = 5.3636$$

The solution of this equation, by means of the false position rule, produces the following:

$$q = 0.850$$
$$\text{Now } q = 1-\text{tg}\alpha \cdot \text{tg}\alpha = 1-q = 0.15$$

In the light of the foregoing considerations, there result the following stick dimensions which, for greater clarity, are shown in tabular form.

Violin Bow

Measured points	Distance along stick in mm	Stick diameter in mm
A	0	8.55
A_0	110	8.55
A_1	220	8.25

Measured points	Distance along stick in mm	Stick diameter in mm
A_2	313.5	7.95
A_3	392.98	7.65
A_4	460.53	7.35
A_5	517.95	7.05
A_6	566.76	6.75
A_7	608.24	6.45
A_8	643.50	6.15
A_9	673.48	5.85
A_{10}	699.0	5.55

Viola Bow

Length of stick excluding head   690 mm
Stick diameter at frog   9 mm
Stick diameter at head   6 mm
The figures shown in the following Table are calculated in the same way as for the violin bow.

Measured points	Distance along stick in mm	Stick diameter in mm
A	0	9
A_0	110	9
A_1	220	8.7
A_2	313.06	8.4
A_3	391.79	8.1

Measured points	Distance along stick in mm	Stick diameter in mm
A_4	458.39	7.8
A_5	514.74	7.5
A_6	562.41	7.2
A_7	602.74	6.9
A_8	636.86	6.6
A_9	665.73	6.3
A_{10}	690.00	6.0

Cello Bow

Length of stick excluding head   665 mm
Stick diameter at frog   10.5 mm
Stick diameter at head   7.5 mm
The cello bow can be sized in the same way as the violin and viola bows.

Measured points	Distance along stick in mm	Stick diameter in mm
A	0	10.5
A_0	105	10.5
A_1	210	10.2
A_2	299.15	9.9
A_3	374.83	9.6
A_4	439.68	9.3
A_5	493.63	9.0
A_6	539.95	8.7
A_7	579.27	8.4

Measured points	Distance along stick in mm	Stick diameter in mm
A_8	612.65	8.1
A_9	640.99	7.8
A_{10}	665.00	7.5

The figures in the foregoing Tables should be regarded as guides. Depending on the material used, bow makers will introduce the appropriate modifications. It is of course necessary to carry out upward or downward rounding off of the figures after the decimal point for practical purposes, e. g., 640.99 is rounded off upwards to 641 mm.

It should be re-emphasized (and the Tables also make this clear) that even if a bow has the correct weight and centre of gravity location it will only be ideal if stick diameter at the centre of gravity is not greater than it is at the start of the stick. Stick diameter can be measured without difficulty by using a slide gauge.

Determining Stick Curvature

The degree to which the hairs can be tightened by the frog screw to tension the bow is a measure of stick quality. In general, a properly tensioned bow, i.e. one ready for playing, should not be more than a stick's thickness away from the hairs at the centre. If the bow is tensioned too heavily for playing there is a risk of breaking off the head. If however it is necessary to tension the bow more than is suggested above, stick curvature has been lost or is defective or alternatively the stick is of poor quality. Tightening the hairs generates a flexural torque with is partly taken up by proper sizing of the cross-section of the stick at the head end

23

(as already mentioned) and partly by flexure of the stick. For this reason, stick curvature should be a parabola whose vertex (or point of maximum flexure) has been shown by experience as best located about 45 cm from the start of the stick. This displacement lends the stick considerably better rigidity. The upper edge of the stick at the frog end must be located in the same plane as the upper edge of the head. This is a prerequisite for a properly curved stick, and the height of the parabola at the point where x = 45 cm should be 1.7−1.8 cm, measured from the upper edge of the stick, for a violin bow. In addition, the stick may not buckle laterally, and this feature is known as stability.

The following example illustrates the calculation of a bow curvature for a stick length of 73 cm − 1 cm = 72 cm, i.e. the length of the violin bow to the centre of the head. The vertex of the curve must be 1.7 cm high at 45 cm along the axis. The foregoing is illustrated by the figure below.

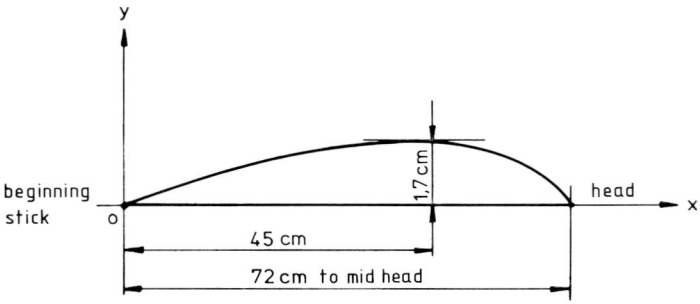

The equations on which this curve is based are somewhat complicated and are therefore omitted here as they are of little interest to practitioners.

Curve Formula

$$Y = - \frac{0.207285}{10000} X^3 + \frac{0.102606}{100} X^2 + \frac{0.335802}{10} X$$

24

All figures for X are shown in cm, and by consequence the figures for Y are also in cm. The foregoing equation produces the following coordinates for stick in a violin bow as defined.

X in cm	Y in cm	Y in mm
0.0	0	0
9.0	0.37	3.7
18.0	0.82	8.2
27.0	1.25	12.5
36.0	1.57	15.7
45.0	1.70	17.0
54.0	1.54	15.4
63.0	1.01	10.1
72.0	0.00	0.0

The following sketch will illustrate the foregoing calculation.

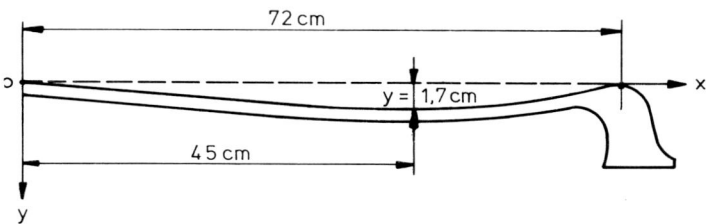

The curve for a viola bow does not depart significantly from that for the violin bow, and no separate calculation is therefore necessary.

Cello Bow

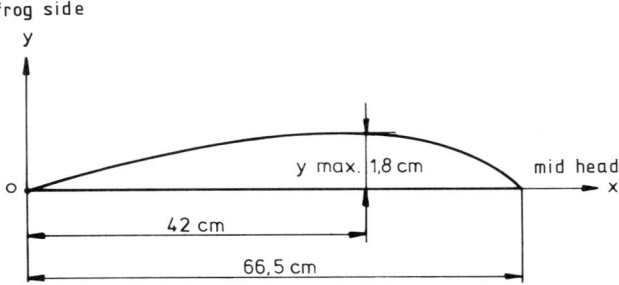

frog side

The foregoing diagram leads to the following curve formula:

$$Y = -\frac{0.297}{10000}\,X^3 + \frac{0.1478}{100}\,X^2 + \frac{0.332}{10}\,X$$

Figures for X are in cm and thus produce figures for Y in cm.
In accordance with the foregoing formula, the following curve
points can be established:

X in cm	Y in cm	Y in mm
0	0	0
6	0.25	2.5
12	0.55	5.5
18	0.90	9.0
24	1.24	12.4
30	1.52	15.2
36	1.725	17.25
42	1.80	18.0
48	1.72	17.2

26

X in cm	Y in cm	Y in mm
54	1.43	14.3
60	0.89	8.9
66.5	0	0

Perfect stick curvature is also a matter of experience and demands considerable intuition on the part of the bow maker.

The foregoing observations would be incomplete without some mention of the bow hairs and hair tensioning device — i.e. the frog and screw — as additional important elements of the bow. However, these can be dealt with very briefly, as no special theoretical aspects are involved.

Bow Hairs

As a rule, horsehair is used, but this is now a rare commodity. Less than 5% of the horsehair produced is suitable for use in first-class bows. Quality depends on length, elasticity, colour and structure and varies considerably. Stallion hairs are stronger, more elastic and longer and are therefore preferred to those from a mare. Bow hair length corresponds roughly to that of the stick. When good horsehair is unobtainable, synthetic hair is also used today. It takes about 5 g of hair to make a violin bow. Affixing the hairs to the bow properly again calls for considerable experience, and defective fixing of the hairs has ruined many an otherwise valuable bow. When properly fitted, a tension to 3 mm should be sufficient to bring the bow to the playing condition. All the hairs must of course lie in a single plane and be evenly tensioned, and the distance between the hairs and the lower edge of the stick at stick centre should under no circumstances be greater than stick diameter at that point, when the bow is ready for playing.

Frog and Screw

The frog and screw are also important elements of a bow and act both as hair tensioning device and counterweight. It is extremely important for the frog to be held centrally in the stick mortise and fit snugly in the channel guides. Frog manufacture and fitment are additional points that demand great skill of a bow maker. To match the quality of the stick and the price of the bow, the materials used may be ebony, ivory or tortoiseshell for the frog, with nickel silver, silver or gold for the mountings.

This booklet does not claim to deal with the immense subject of bows exhaustively. Its aim is to give outsiders some idea of the complexity of the subject.

Embrach (Switzerland) March, 1981